With a few common materials you can provide 36 delightful board games for your second grade classroom. These games are designed to provide important practice for children learning their math facts and algorithms. Hopefully these games will help children memorize their facts in an enjoyable, yet effective, way and be substituted for some of the skill practice sheets that are often provided. The games are designed to be easy to learn, with directions provided on each game board—a perfect choice for learning centers when students must work independently. If you are searching for ways to involve parents or guardians in their children's math experiences, create "math take-home game kits" by mounting the game boards on file folders and attaching small envelopes for game pieces. The games can be used as "homework" assignments—to be played with an adult or older child at home. They can also be sent home for extra practice when parents request helpful materials or when you feel it is needed. Children may even choose to play one of these games at recess or during free time. If you are searching for curriculum materials for after-school programs, summer school programs, or neighborhood center programs, these game materials require minimal preparation.

Before distributing the game materials to students, read the game directions ahead of time and prepare the materials as needed. Most of the games use "cards" that are supplied at the end of *Math Practice Games Grade 2* and indicated in the game directions. To prepare the game cards, photocopy the pattern pages, then cut apart the cards. As you prepare the game boards and cards, be sure to consider these possibilities:
- Copy the game board and cards on construction paper so they will last longer. This way the problem cannot be read through the back of the card.
- Enlarge the game board and/or cards if the school copier uses 11" x 17" (279 x 432 mm) paper.
- Laminate the game materials for durability.

Most games also need game markers for the children to use. The game markers must fit in the spaces as indicated on the game board. They must also be easy for children to pick up. Different colors or kinds must be available so the players can distinguish their game markers from their opponents. It is possible to use crayons instead of game markers on many game boards, however, by using game markers the cost for producing the games is minimal and less paper is used in the long run. Here are some items that could be used as game markers:
- counters
- buttons
- macaroni
- paper clips
- candy pieces
- dried beans
- centimeter cubes
- wads or squares of construction paper
- Styrofoam packing materials
- game markers from commercial games

Undoubtedly, you will be able to add to this list!

Math Practice Games Grade 2 can be used in many different ways. If a game is being introduced to the whole class, reproduce the game board on a transparency and use the overhead projector when explaining the game rules. Some teachers may prefer to introduce a game to a math group and have just that group use it. At times, a game may simply be given to a pair or group of children who can read the directions and follow them on their own. If a child cannot read the directions, he or she can be paired with someone who can.

When children are playing a game, they should be expected to check each other's answers and to use scratch paper if necessary. Figuring out fact answers mentally or memorizing them is the goal at some point. The game cards can be used as flash cards or even as timed tests for straightforward practice of memorization.

Hopefully the materials in *Math Practice Games Grade 2* will become a useful part of your overall math program and provide delightful math experiences for children who have not yet mastered their facts or computation skills.

BAT A HOME RUN!

Players: 2

Object: To cover a bat with 4 game markers

Other Materials: Game markers or different color crayon for each player, Cards A and B

To Play:
1. Mix up the cards and place them *face down* in a pile.
2. Each player takes a card, calls out the answer, and marks one of the spaces with the correct answer.
3. If no answer is left, the player loses that turn.
4. Keep on playing until someone marks one whole bat to hit a home run.

2 1 8 5	6 3 7 9
9 4 7 6	10 2 7 5
7 6 10 8	8 10 5 10
4 5 0 6	10 9 8 2
3 8 6 9	8 10 3 9
8 4 9 10	7 4 9 10

© Instructional Fair • TS Denison

IF5204 *Math Practice Games Gr. 2*

FACT-TAC-TOE

Players: 2

Object: To cover 3 spaces in a row

Other Materials: Cards C, game markers for each player

To Play:
1. Mix up the cards and place them *face down* in a pile.
2. Each player takes a card, reads the number, and places a game marker on one of the spaces with a problem that has the same answer.
3. Keep on playing until someone has 3 markers in a →, ↓ or ↗ row.
4. Play again. Keep track of who wins each time.

0 + 8	1 + 1	0 + 4
4 + 4	3 + 3	1 + 9
1 + 5	0 + 0	2 + 5

3 + 7	2 + 2	1 + 6
4 + 5	0 + 1	3 + 4
2 + 6	1 + 2	0 + 7

0 + 5	2 + 3	1 + 3
1 + 7	3 + 5	0 + 2
0 + 9	5 + 5	2 + 7

3 + 6	0 + 6	2 + 4
4 + 6	1 + 4	1 + 8
0 + 3	2 + 8	0 + 10

GHOST BINGO

Players: 2

Object: The first player to have 4 markers in a row is the winner.

Other Materials: Cards A and B, game markers for each player

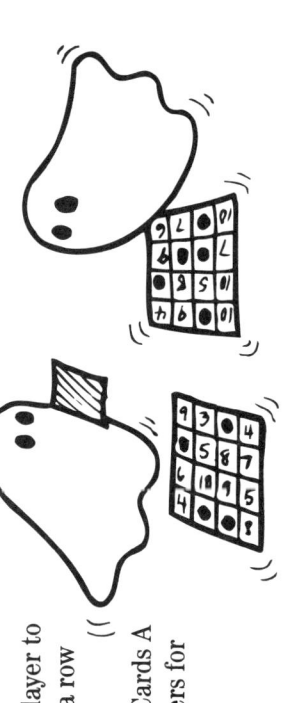

To Play:

1. Mix up the cards and place them *face down* in a pile.
2. Each player chooses a bingo board.
3. Each player draws a card, calls out the answer, and marks one of the ghosts with the correct answer on his or her bingo board.
4. If no answer is left, the player loses that turn.
5. Keep on playing until someone covers 4 ghosts in a →, ↓ or ↗ row.
6. Play again. Keep track of who wins each time.

Name ______________________

9	3	6	4
7	5	8	7
6	10	9	5
4	8	10	8

Name ______________________

10	8	9	4
10	5	8	6
7	10	3	9
10	9	7	6

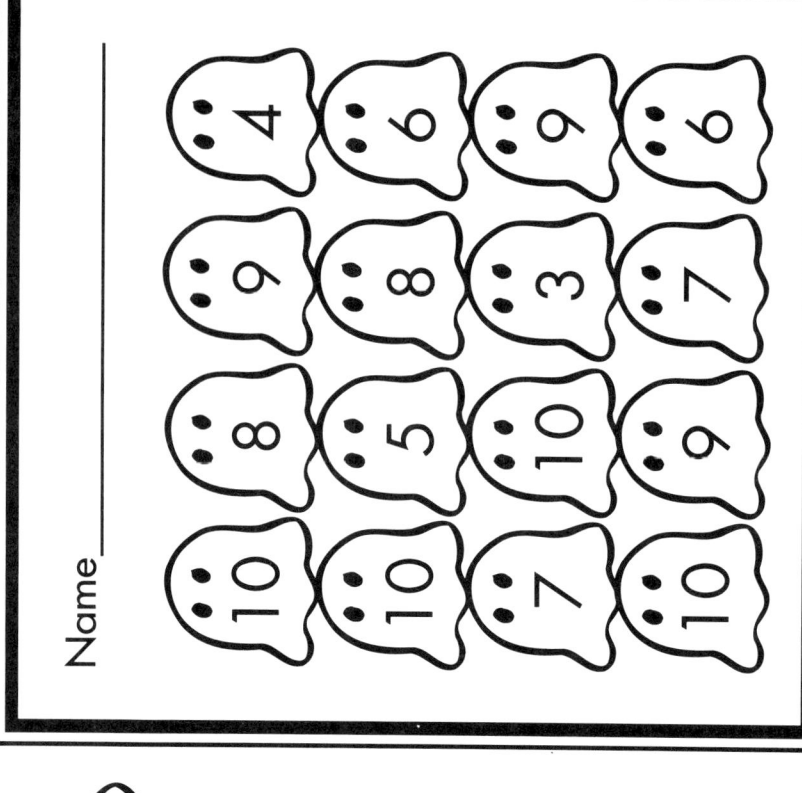

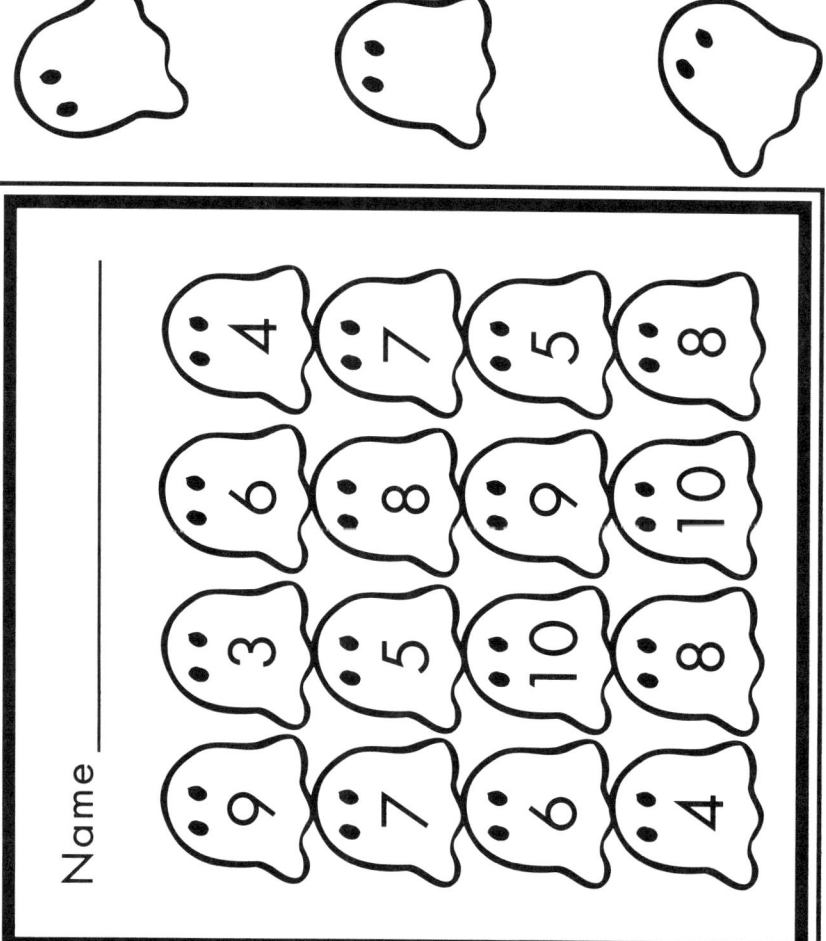

NUMBER MAZE

Players: 2

Object: To reach the "Winner" box

Other Materials: Cards D and E, game marker for each player

To Play:
1. Mix up the cards and place them *face down* in a pile.
2. Each player places a game marker at "Start."
3. Players take turns drawing a card and moving a game marker to the first correct answer.
4. If the first correct answer is already marked, the player loses that turn.
5. Keep on playing until someone gets to the "Winner" box.

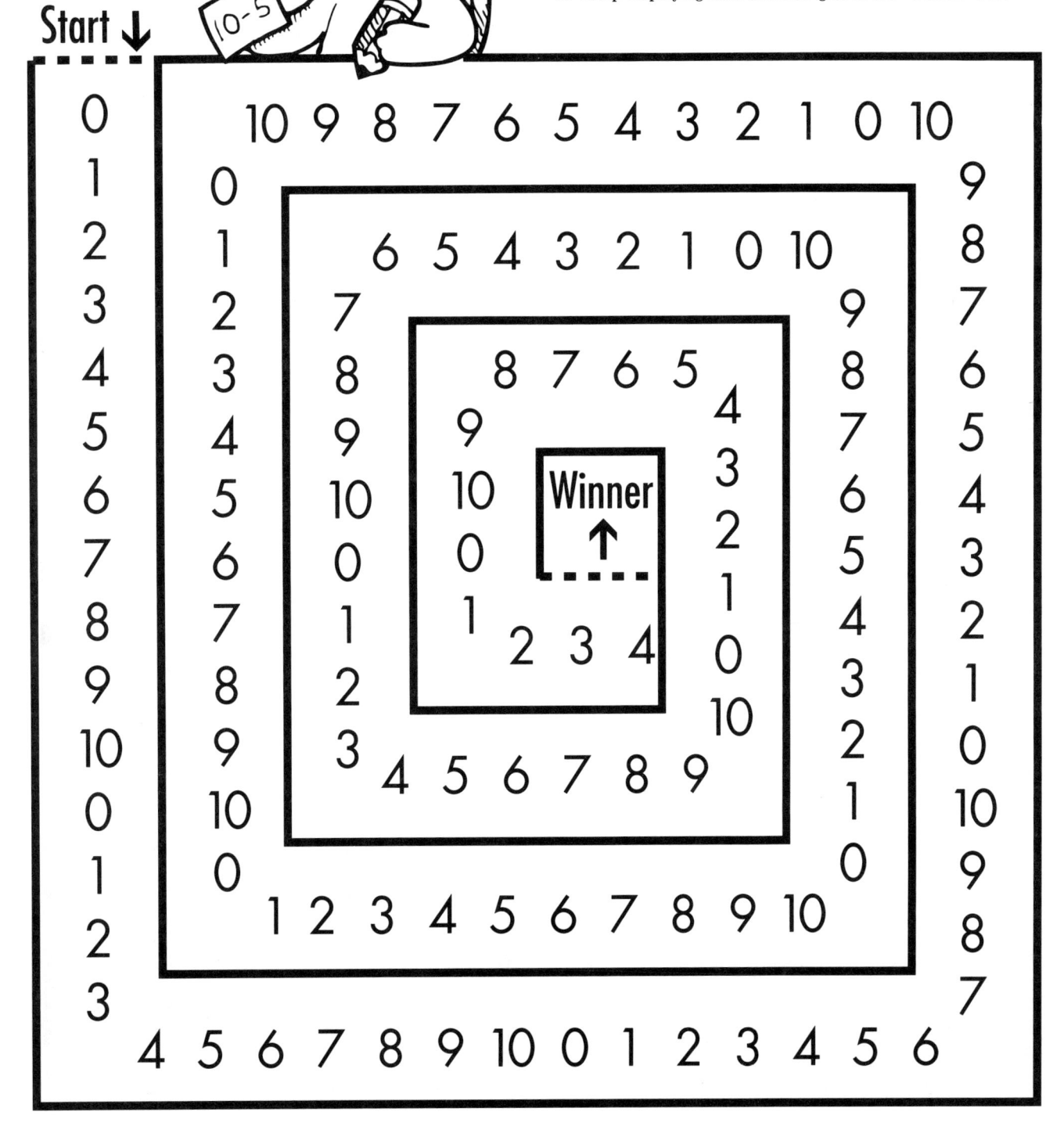

RETURN OF FACT-TAC-TOE

Players: 2

Object: To cover 3 spaces in a row

Other Materials: Cards C, game markers for each player

To Play:
1. Mix up the cards and place them *face down* in a pile.
2. Each player takes a card, reads the number, and places a game marker on one of the spaces with a problem that has the same answer.
3. Keep on playing until someone has 3 markers in a →, ↓ or ↗ row.
4. Play again. Keep track of who wins each time.

9 – 3	7 – 5	3 – 2
8 – 7	4 – 3	10 –
6 – 2	10 –	6 – 4

7 – 2	8 – 4	5 – 3
6 – 5	10 – 5	4 – 2
10 –	8 – 3	9 – 5

10 – 3	7 – 6	6 – 3
9 – 8	5 – 2	8 – 5
7 – 4	9 – 2	10 – 7

10 –	9 – 6	5 – 4
10 – 9	8 – 6	8 – 2
7 – 3	9 – 4	9 – 7

© Instructional Fair • TS Denison   IF5204 *Math Practice Games Gr. 2*

FACE BINGO

Players: 2

Object: The first player to cover 4 faces in a row is the winner.

Other Materials: Cards D and E, game markers for each player

To Play:
1. Mix up the cards and place them *face down* in a pile.
2. Each player chooses a bingo board.
3. Each player draws a card, calls out the answer, and marks one of the faces with the correct answer on his or her bingo board.
4. If no answer is left, the player loses a turn.
5. Keep on playing until someone covers 4 faces in a →, ↓ or ↗ row.
6. Play again. Keep track of who wins each time.

Name _____

0	5	2	1
2	6	9	1
3	6	0	4
4	7	8	3

Name _____

2	1	8	3
2	6	7	1
5	3	0	4
0	5	10	7

COLOR A COW

Players: 2

Object: To place 4 markers on top of a cow

Other Materials: Game markers or different color crayon for each player, Cards A, B, D, and E

To Play:
1. Mix up the cards and place them *face down* in a pile.
2. Each player takes a card, calls out the answer, and marks one of the spots with the correct answer.
3. If no answer is left, the player loses that turn.
4. Continue playing until someone marks one whole cow.

© Instructional Fair • TS Denison

8

IF5204 *Math Practice Games Gr. 2*

FETCH THE FRIES

Players: 2

Object: The first player to cover his or her fries is the winner.

Other Materials: Game markers or color crayon for each player, Cards A, B, D, and E

To Play:
1. Mix up the cards and place them *face down* in a pile.
2. Each player draws a card, calls out the answer, and covers one of the fries with that answer in his or her container.
3. If no answer is left, the player loses that turn.
4. Continue playing until someone has marked all fries.

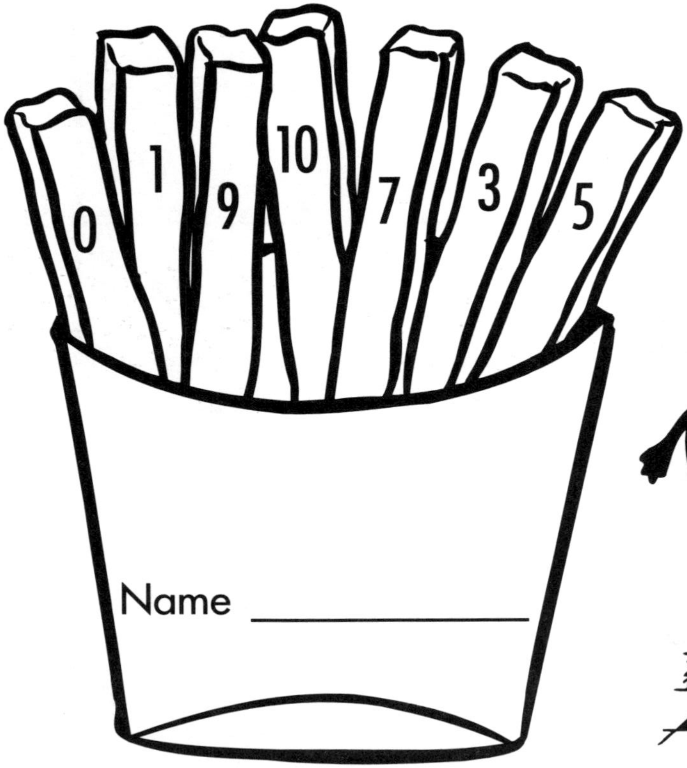

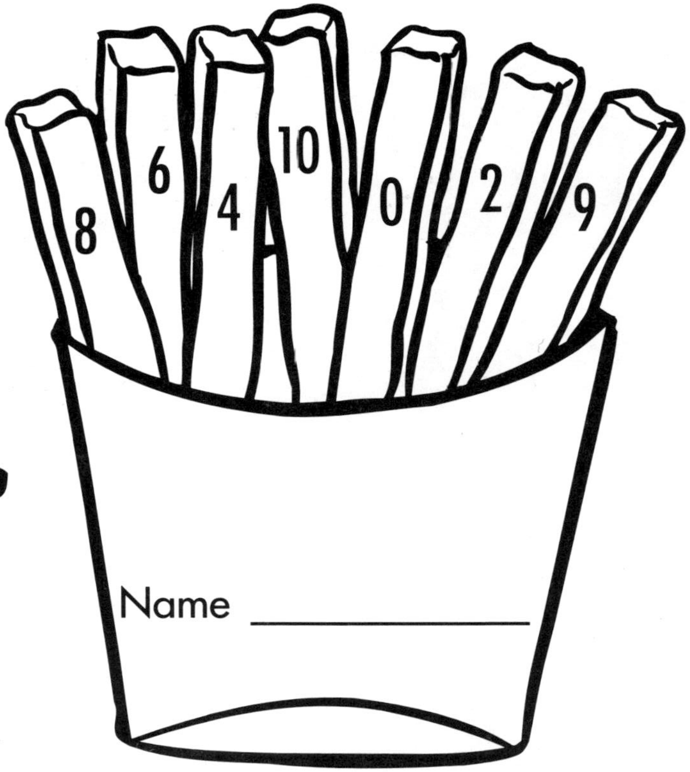

DRAGON BINGO

Players: Entire class

Object: The first player to mark 4 squares in a row is the winner.

Other Materials: Game markers, Cards A, B, D, and E

Prepare: Give each player a copy of the bingo board.

To Play:
1. Mix up the cards and place them *face down* in a pile.
2. The teacher draws a card and calls out the problem or writes it on the chalkboard.
3. Each player marks one of the squares with the correct answer.
4. Continue playing until someone covers 4 squares in a →, ↓ or ↗ row.

10	6	7	0	4	3
9	5	3	2	6	8
4	1	4	5	9	10
2	8	0	7	1	6
6	5	9	2	3	5
8	1	7	4	10	0

TOWER OF FACTS

Players: 2

Object: The first player to cover her or his tower is the winner.

Other Materials: Cards F (without "9 + 9")

To Play:
1. Mix up the cards and place them *face down* in a pile.
2. Each player draws a card, calls out the answer, and places the card on the correct number on the tower.
3. If no answer is left, the player loses that turn.
4. Keep on playing until someone covers all the answers on her or his tower.
5. Play again. Keep track of who wins each time.

Name _____

Name _____

COLLECT FOUR FACTS

problem	problem
answer	answer

problem	problem
answer	answer

Name _____

Players: 2
Object: The first player to cover his or her boxes is the winner.
Other Materials: Cards G

To Play:
1. Mix up the cards and place them *face down* in a pile.
2. Each player draws a card and then draws another one.
3. Keep on drawing cards, arranging them *face up* in the playing area.
4. When both a problem and its answer have been drawn, the player places those cards on the game board.
5. Continue playing until someone has all his or her boxes covered.

problem	problem
answer	answer

problem	problem
answer	answer

Name _____

© Instructional Fair • TS Denison

IF5204 *Math Practice Games Gr. 2*

FLOWER BINGO

Players: 2

Object: The first player to cover 4 flowers in a row is the winner.

Other Materials: Cards F, game markers for each player

To Play:
1. Mix up the cards and place them *face down* in a pile.
2. Each player draws a card, calls out the answer, and marks one of the flowers with the correct answer on his or her bingo board.
3. If no answer is left, the player loses that turn.
4. Keep on playing until someone covers 4 flowers in a →, ↓ or ↗ row.
5. Play again. Keep track of who wins each time.

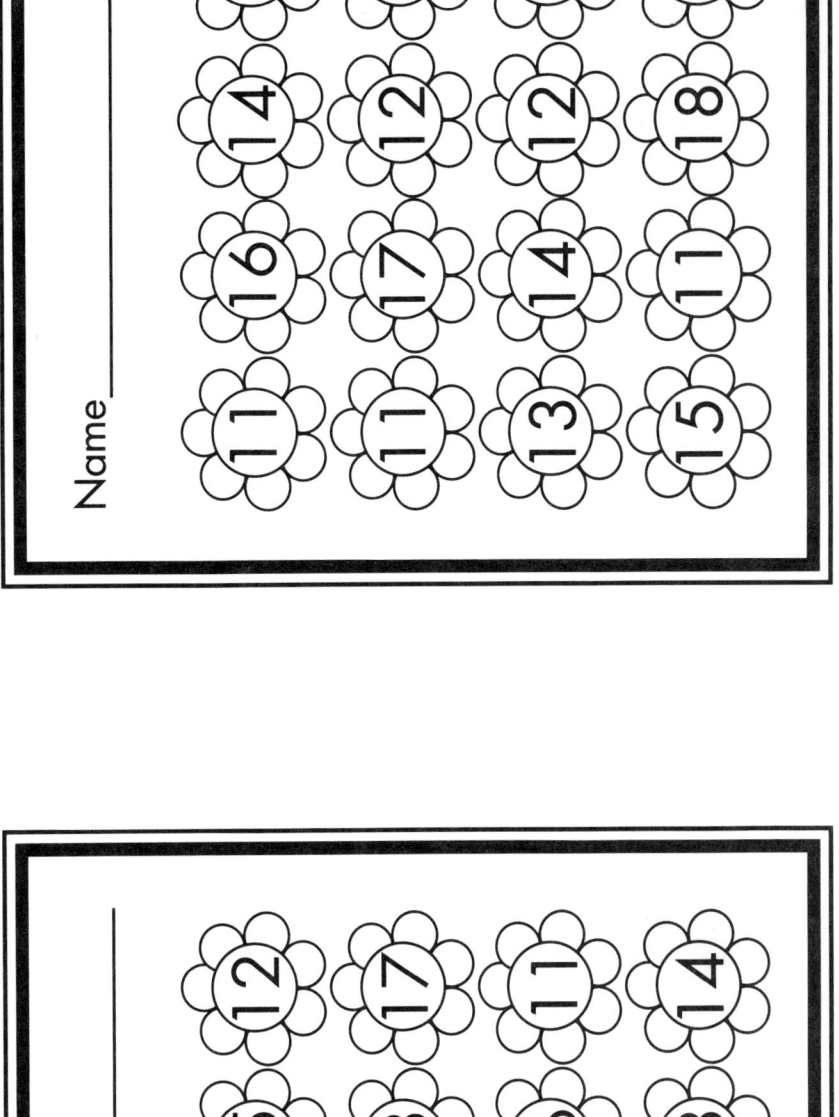

© Instructional Fair • TS Denison   13   IF5204 *Math Practice Games Gr. 2*

Players: 1, 2, 3, or entire class
Object: To match all problem cards with answers
Other Materials: Cards F

Prepare: Give each player an enlarged copy of the game board and set of cards.
To Play:
1. Mix up the cards and place them *face down*.
2. Players start at the same time. Each player draws cards and matches them on top of the answers.
3. Game ends when all cards are matched.

PROBLEM MATCH RACE

11	12	13	14	15	18
11	12	13	14	15	17
11	12	13	14	15	17
11	12	12	13	15	16
11	11	12	13	14	16
11	11	12	13	14	16

© Instructional Fair • TS Denison

IF5204 *Math Practice Games Gr. 2*

NUMBER CASTLE

Players: 2

Object: To reach "Out"

Other Materials: Cards H, different color crayon or game marker for each player

To Play:
1. Mix up the cards and place them *face down* in a pile.
2. Each player places a game marker at "In."
3. Each player draws a card, calls out the answer, and marks the first correct number.
4. If that number is already marked, the player loses that turn.
5. Play continues until someone gets to "Out."

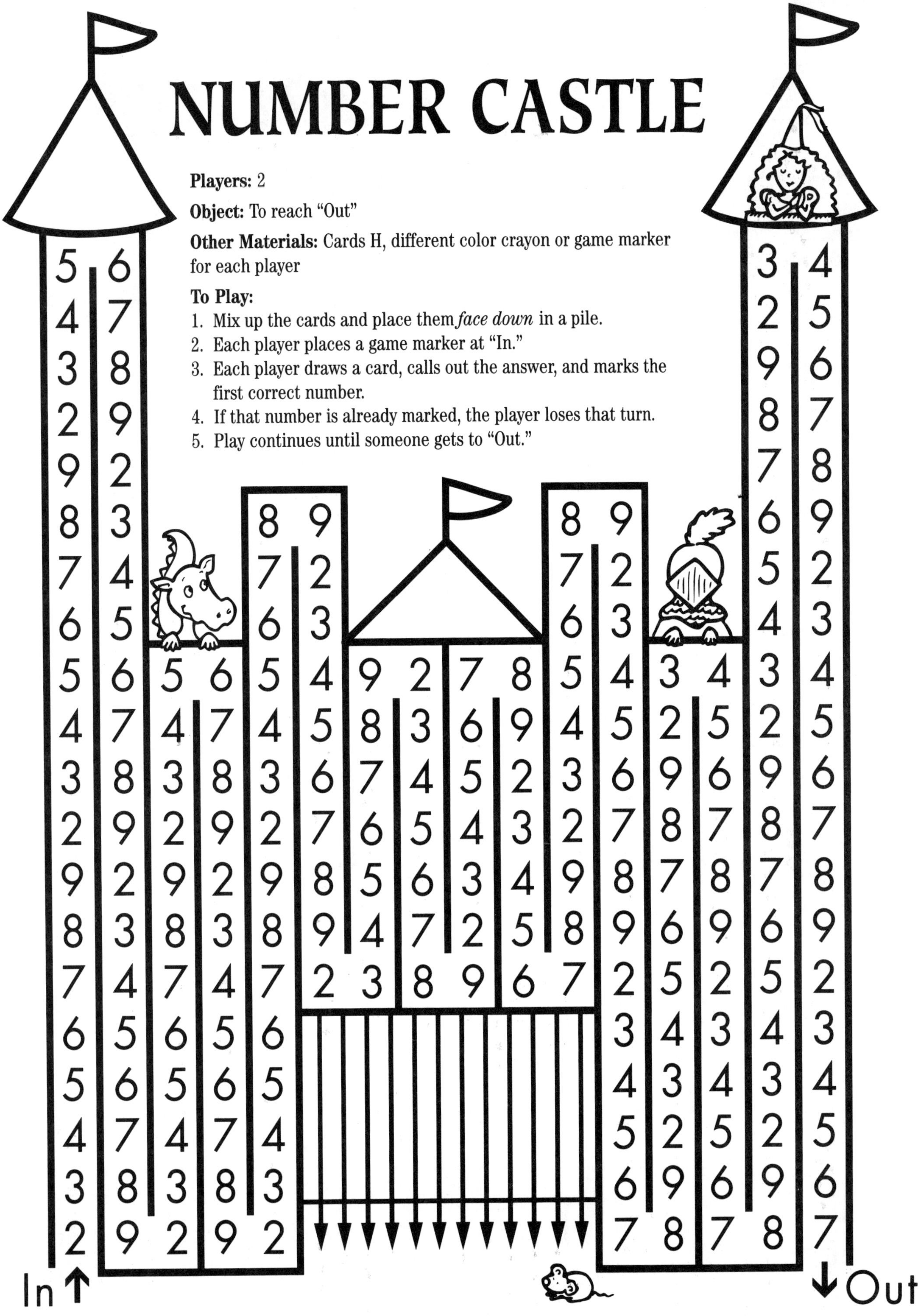

In ↑   ↓ Out

SUBTRACT NINE-TAC-TOE

Players: 2

Object: To cover 3 spaces in a row

Other Materials: Cards C, game markers for each player

To Play:
1. Mix up the cards and place them *face down* in a pile.
2. Each player takes a card, reads the number, and places a game marker on the space with a problem that has the same answer.
3. If no problem matches, the player loses that turn.
4. Keep on playing until someone has 3 markers in a →, ↓ or ↗ row.
5. Play again. Keep track of who wins each time.

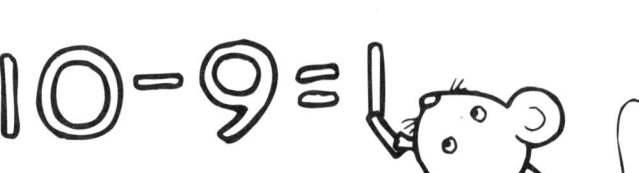

Name _____

15 – 9	12 – 9	17 – 9
16 – 9	18 – 9	11 – 9
13 – 9	14 – 9	10 – 9

Name _____

15 – 9	18 – 9	14 – 9
10 – 9	12 – 9	16 – 9
17 – 9	11 – 9	13 – 9

KITE BINGO

Players: 2
Object: The first player to mark 4 kites in a row is the winner.
Other Materials: Cards H, game markers for each player

To Play:
1. Mix up the cards and place them *face down* in a pile.
2. Each player draws a card, calls out the answer, and marks one of the kites with the correct answer on his or her bingo board.
3. If no answer is left, the player loses that turn.
4. Continue playing until someone covers 4 kites in a →, ↓ or ↗ row.
5. Play again. Keep track of who wins each time.

Players: 1, 2, 3, or entire class

Object: To match all problem cards with answers

Other Materials: Cards H

Prepare: Give each player an enlarged copy of the game board and set of cards.

To Play:

1. Mix up the cards and place them *face down*.
2. Players start at the same time. Each player draws cards and matches them on top of the answers.
3. Game ends when all cards are matched.

ANOTHER PROBLEM MATCH RACE

2	3	3	4	4	4
5	5	5	5	6	6
6	6	6	7	7	7
7	7	7	8	8	8
8	8	8	8	9	9
9	9	9	9	9	9

COLLECT THE BONES

Players: 2

Object: Be the first player to place 3 game markers on bones. The player with the most points is the winner.

Other Materials: Cards A, B, and F, game markers or different color crayon for each player

To Play:
1. Mix up the cards and place them *face down* in a pile.
2. Each player takes a card, calls out the answer, and marks one of the spaces with the correct number.
3. If no answer is left, the player loses that turn.
4. Continue until all spaces are marked. Whoever has more bones covered is the winner.

© Instructional Fair • TS Denison

19

IF5204 *Math Practice Games Gr. 2*

MOON TRIP

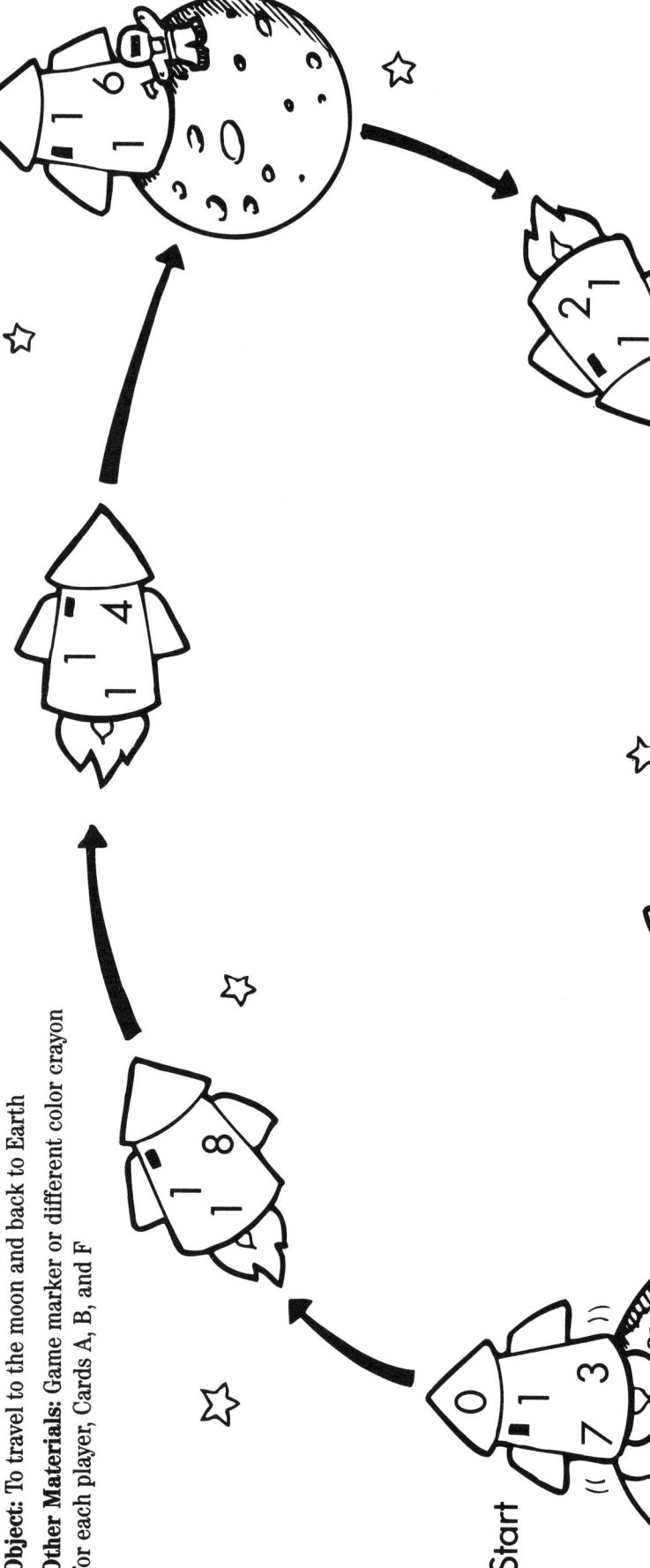

Players: 2 or more
Object: To travel to the moon and back to Earth
Other Materials: Game marker or different color crayon for each player, Cards A, B, and F

To Play:
1. Mix up the cards and place them *face down* in a pile.
2. Each player draws a card, calls out the answer, and places a marker on the "Start" rocket if the answer is shown.
3. If the answer is not shown, the player loses that turn.
4. Each player must make the trip one rocket at a time and return to the "Start" rocket.
5. Keep on playing until someone returns to Earth first.

© Instructional Fair • TS Denison   IF5204 *Math Practice Games Gr. 2*

HIPPO BINGO

Players: Entire class

Object: The first player to cover 4 squares in a row is the winner.

Other Materials: Game markers for each player; Cards A, B, and F

Prepare: Give each player a copy of the bingo board.

To Play:
1. Mix up the cards and place them *face down* in a pile.
2. The teacher draws a card and calls out the problem or writes it on the chalkboard.
3. Each player marks one of the squares with the correct answer on the bingo board.
4. Keep on playing until someone covers 4 squares in a ←, ↑, or ↗ row.

7	1	14	6	12	2
16	18	0	15	11	8
10	5	12	14	3	13
15	8	11	2	5	10
3	9	7	16	1	4
17	4	9	13	6	0

© Instructional Fair • TS Denison

IF5204 *Math Practice Games Gr. 2*

BALLOON RIDE

Players: 2

Object: To place 4 markers on top of a balloon

Other Materials: Game markers or different color crayon for each player, Cards D, E, and H (without "10 – 0")

To Play:
1. Mix up the cards and place them *face down* in a pile.
2. Each player takes a card, calls out the answer, and marks one of the spaces with the correct answer.
3. If no answer is left, the player loses that turn.
4. Keep on playing until someone marks one whole balloon.

CATCH THE MONSTER

Players: 2

Object: The first player to cover his/her monster is the winner.

Other Materials: Game markers for each player, Cards D, E, and H

To Play:
1. Mix up the cards and place them *face down* in a pile.
2. Each player draws a card, calls out the answer, and places it on the correct number on his or her monster.
3. If no answer is left or if the answer is not shown, the player loses that turn.
4. Keep on playing until someone covers all the answers.
5. Play again. Keep track of who wins each time.

Name _____

Name _____

BITE BINGO

Players: Entire class

Object: The first player to cover 4 squares in a row is the winner.

Other Materials: Game markers for each player, Cards D, E, and H (without "10 – 0")

Prepare: Give each player a copy of the bingo board.

To Play:
1. Mix up the cards and place them *face down* in a pile.
2. The teacher draws a card and calls out the problem or writes it on the chalkboard.
3. Each player marks one of the squares with the correct answer on his or her bingo board.
4. Keep on playing until someone covers 4 squares in a →, ↓ or ↗ row.

4	5	0	1	3	5
2	7	8	2	6	8
8	1	5	9	4	2
6	0	7	0	3	5
1	3	6	4	1	3
9	4	2	9	7	0

FIVE ON A SNAKE

Players: 2 or 3

Object: To mark 5 numbers in a row

Other Materials: Game markers or different color crayon for each player, Cards A, B, D, E, F, and H

To Play:
1. Mix up the cards and place them *face down* in a pile.
2. Each player draws a card, calls out the answer, and marks one of the spaces with the correct answer.
3. If no answer is left, the player loses that turn.
4. Continue playing until someone marks 5 numbers in a row.

SUNKEN TREASURE

Players: 2 or more
Object: To reach the treasure
Other Materials: Cards A, B, D, E, F, and H, game marker for each player

To Play:
1. Mix up the cards and place them *face down* in a pile.
2. Each player starts at the diver.
3. Each player draws a card, calls out the answer, and moves to Level 1 if the answer is shown.
4. If the answer is not shown, the player loses that turn.
5. Each player must make the dive one level at a time.
6. Continue playing until someone reaches the treasure.

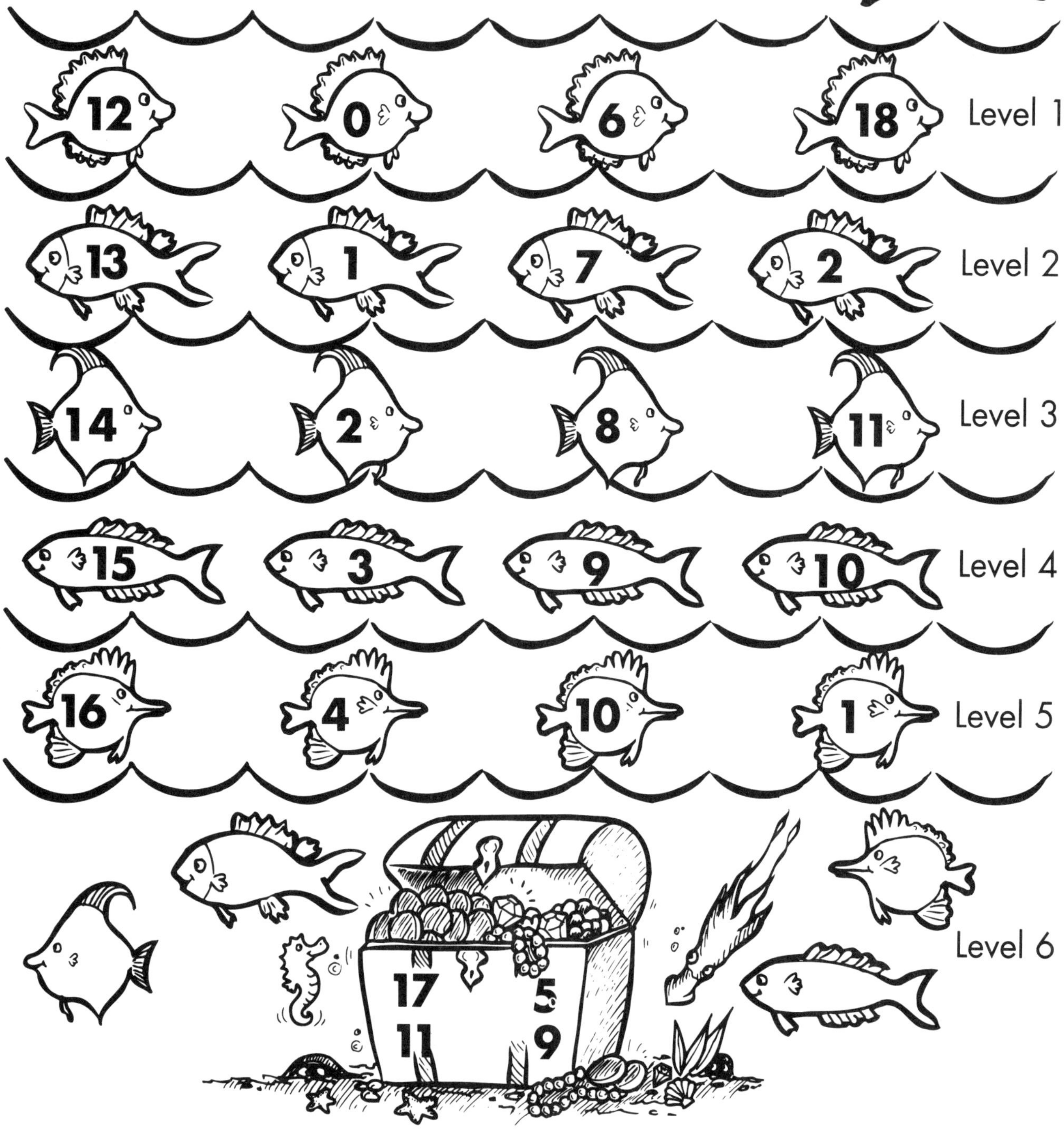

12 0 6 18 Level 1
13 1 7 2 Level 2
14 2 8 11 Level 3
15 3 9 10 Level 4
16 4 10 1 Level 5

17 5 11 9 Level 6

VOLCANO BINGO

Players: Entire class
Object: To cover 4 squares in a row
Other Materials: Game markers for each player, Cards A, B, D, E, F, and H
Prepare: Give each player a copy of the bingo board.

To Play:
1. Mix up the cards and place them *face down* in a pile.
2. The teacher draws a card and calls out the problem or writes it on the chalkboard.
3. Each player marks one of the squares with the correct answer on his or her bingo board.
4. Keep on playing until someone covers 4 squares in a →, ↓ or ↗ row.

9	11	15	3	4	13
18	5	7	12	10	8
13	16	3	14	1	6
9	15	9	7	2	4
2	11	1	17	10	12
5	14	6	8	0	16

PLACE VALUE BINGO

Players: 2
Object: To mark 4 boxes in a row
Other Materials: Game markers or different color crayon for each player, Cards I, J, and K

To Play:
1. Mix up the cards and place them *face down* in a pile.
2. Each player draws a card and marks one box with a number and place value that matches the card.
3. If no answer is left, the player loses that turn.
4. A "Wild Card" may be played anywhere.
5. Keep on playing until someone covers 4 boxes in a →, ↓ or ↗ row.

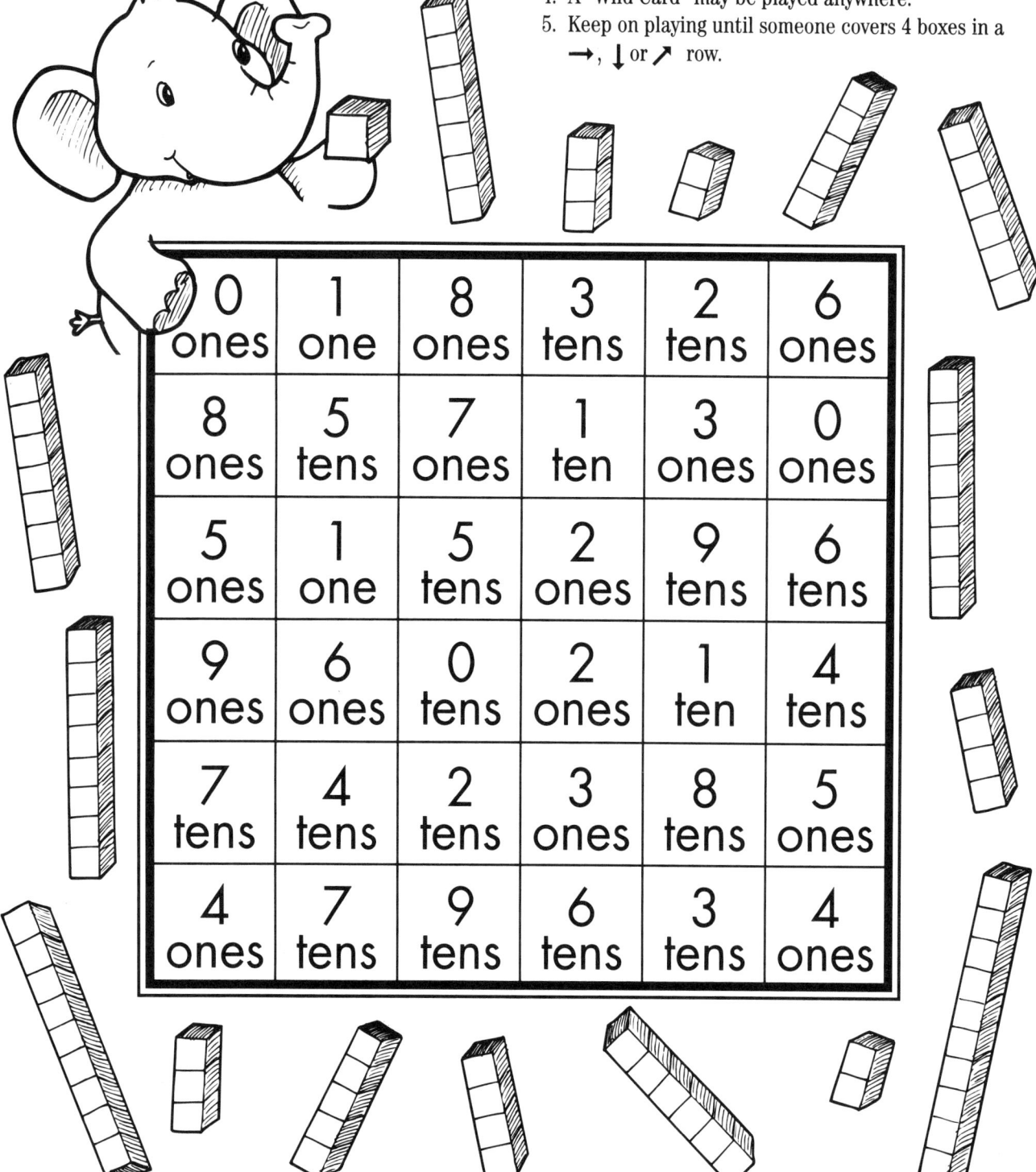

0 ones	1 one	8 ones	3 tens	2 tens	6 ones
8 ones	5 tens	7 ones	1 ten	3 ones	0 ones
5 ones	1 one	5 tens	2 ones	9 tens	6 tens
9 ones	6 ones	0 tens	2 ones	1 ten	4 tens
7 tens	4 tens	2 tens	3 ones	8 tens	5 ones
4 ones	7 tens	9 tens	6 tens	3 tens	4 ones

BIG-TAC-TOE

Players: 2

Object: To cover 3 boxes in a row

Other Materials: Game markers for each player, pencil, Cards I, J, and K (without "Wild Cards")

To Play:
1. Mix up the cards and place them *face down* in a pile.
2. Each player draws a card and marks one box that goes with the number on the card.
3. The players take turns. If no answer is left, the player loses that turn.
4. Keep on playing until someone covers 3 boxes in a →, ↓ or ↗ row.
5. Play again. Shade a box below for each win. Whoever wins 10 rounds first is the champion.

Under 50	Over 50	Under 70
Between 50 and 70	Over 30	Under 30
Over 70	Between 30 and 50	Between 70 and 90

Name _____

Name _____

TREE HOUSE RACE

Players: 2

Object: To reach the tree house

Other Materials: Game marker for each player, Cards I, J, and K (without "Wild Cards")

To Play:
1. Mix up the cards and place them *face down* in a pile.
2. Each player places a game marker at "Start."
3. Each player takes a card and reads the number. Players compare the two numbers.
4. The player with the higher number moves his or her game marker up one rung on the ladder.
5. Keep on playing until someone reaches the tree house.

FILL UP TWO BOXES

Players: 2 or more

Object: To cover 2 boxes with cards

Other Materials: Game markers for each player, Cards I, J, and K (without "Wild Cards")

Prepare: Give each player a copy of this page.

To Play:
1. Mix up the cards and place them *face down* in a pile.
2. Each player takes a card and places it in the correct box on his or her game board.
3. If there is not an empty space for a card, the player loses that turn.
4. Keep on playing until someone fills 2 boxes with cards.

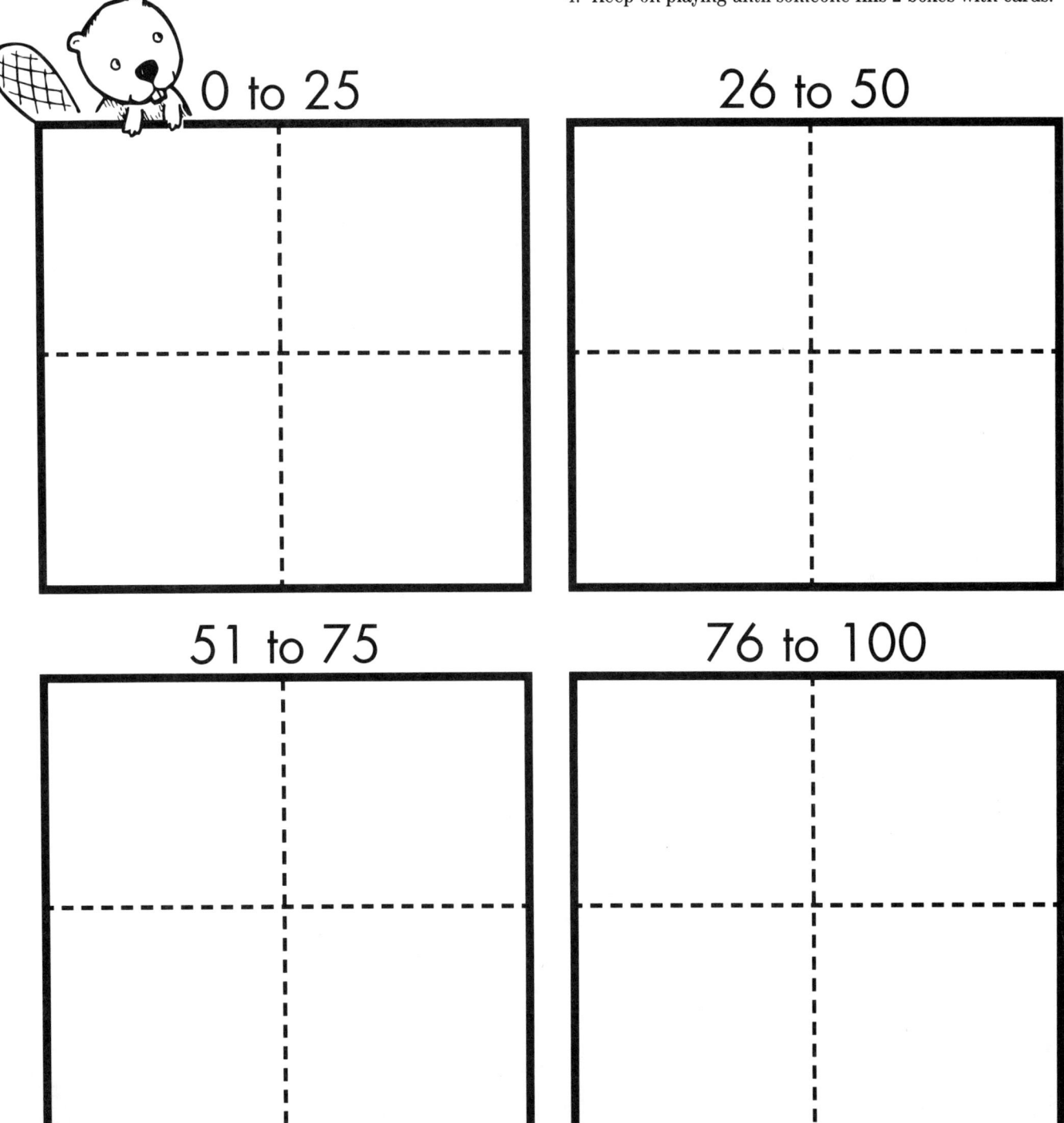

Bowl a Strike!

Players: 2

Object: To mark 10 pins for a strike

Other Materials: Game markers or different color crayon for each player, Cards I, J, and K

To Play:
1. Place the cards *face down* and mix them up.
2. Each player takes 2 cards, adds, and marks the pin with that answer.
3. If no number is left, the player loses that turn.
4. If a "Wild Card" is drawn, the player may save it.
5. Keep on playing until someone marks all of her or his pins. A "Wild Card" may be used to mark the last pin to win.

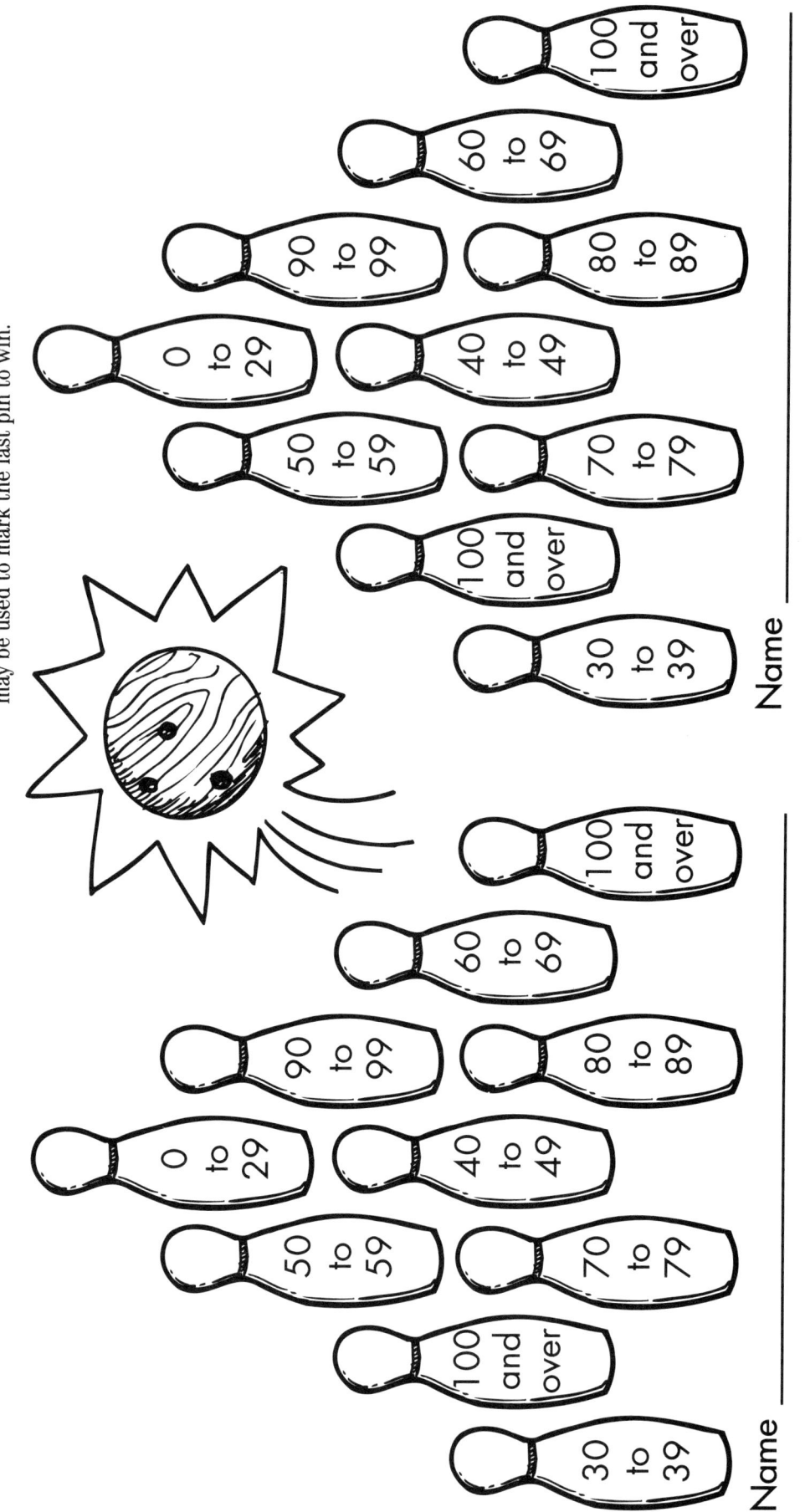

Name

Name

ADDITION—THREE IN A ROW

Players: 2

Object: To place 3 markers in a row

Other Materials: Game markers or different color crayon for each player, Cards I and J (without "Wild Cards")

To Play:
1. Mix up the cards and place them *face down* in a pile.
2. Each player takes 2 cards, adds, and marks the square with that answer.
3. If the answer is 100 or higher or if it is already marked, the player loses that turn.
4. Keep on playing until someone marks 3 squares in a →, ↓ or ↗ row.

0	1	2	3	4	5	6	7	8	9
10	11	12	13	14	15	16	17	18	19
20	21	22	23	24	25	26	27	28	29
30	31	32	33	34	35	36	37	38	39
40	41	42	43	44	45	46	47	48	49
50	51	52	53	54	55	56	57	58	59
60	61	62	63	64	65	66	67	68	69
70	71	72	73	74	75	76	77	78	79
80	81	82	83	84	85	86	87	88	89
90	91	92	93	94	95	96	97	98	99

© Instructional Fair • TS Denison

EAT A WHOLE PIE!

Players: 2

Object: The first player to cover all spaces on a pie is the winner.

Other Materials: Game markers for each player, Cards I, J, and K

To Play:
1. Mix up the cards and place them *face down* in a pile.
2. Each player takes 2 cards, subtracts, and marks the slice with that answer.
3. If no answer is left, the player loses that turn.
4. If a "Wild Card" is drawn, the player may save it.
5. Keep on playing until someone marks all of his or her slices. A "Wild Card" may be used to mark the last slice to win.

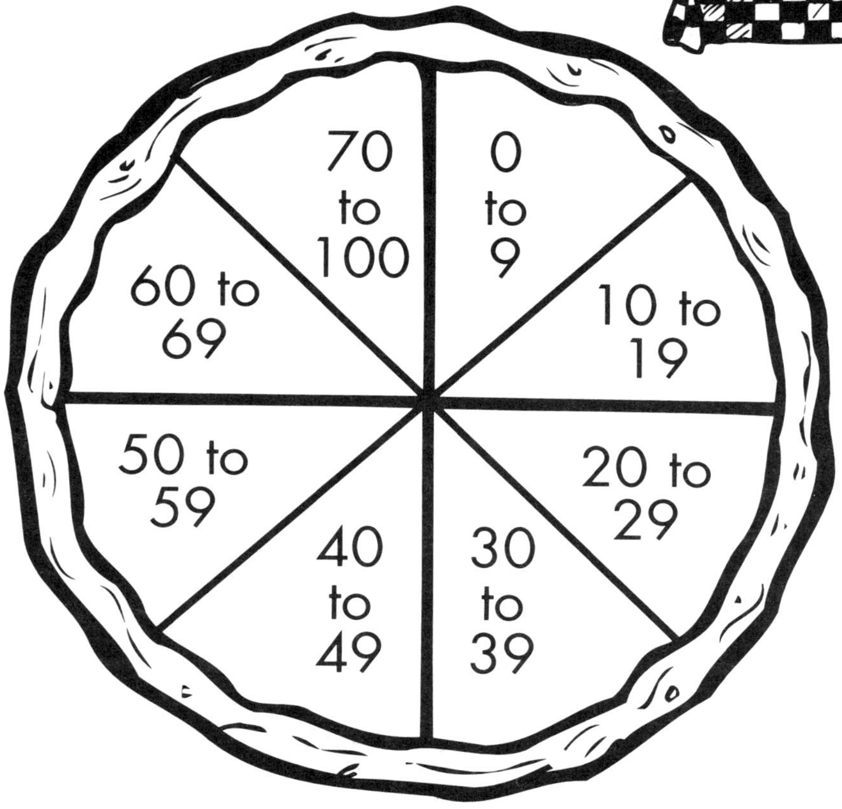

Name _____

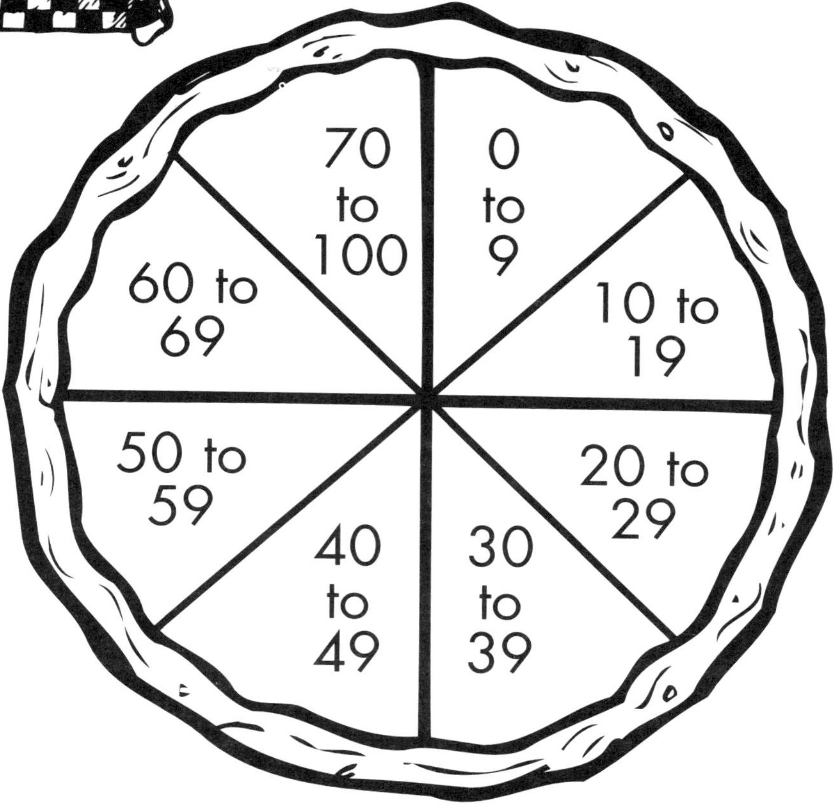

Name _____

SUBTRACTION-THREE IN A ROW

Players: 2

Object: To place 3 markers in a row

Other Materials: Game markers or different color crayon for each player, Cards I, J, and K (without "Wild Cards")

To Play:
1. Mix up the cards and place them *face down* in a pile.
2. Each player takes 2 cards, subtracts, and marks the square with that answer.
3. If the answer is already marked, the player loses that turn.
4. Keep on playing until someone marks 3 squares in a →, ↓ or ↗ row.

0	1	2	3	4	5	6	7	8	9
10	11	12	13	14	15	16	17	18	19
20	21	22	23	24	25	26	27	28	29
30	31	32	33	34	35	36	37	38	39
40	41	42	43	44	45	46	47	48	49
50	51	52	53	54	55	56	57	58	59
60	61	62	63	64	65	66	67	68	69
70	71	72	73	74	75	76	77	78	79
80	81	82	83	84	85	86	87	88	89
90	91	92	93	94	95	96	97	98	99

© Instructional Fair • TS Denison   IF5204 *Math Practice Games Gr. 2*

ICE CREAM EATING CONTEST

Players: 2

Object: To mark 3 spaces on an ice cream cone

Other Materials: Game markers or different color crayon for each player, scissors

Preparation: Cut out the number cards shown below.

To Play:
1. Mix up the cards and place them *face down* in a pile.
2. Each player takes 2 cards, multiplies, and marks the answer on an ice cream cone.
3. If no answer is left, the player loses that turn.
4. When all cards have been used, mix them up and use them again.
5. Keep on playing until someone marks a whole ice cream cone.

Cones (top row): 18/20/5, 12/4/6, 16/4/0, 25/10/5, 3/20/12

Cones (bottom row): 36/8/6, 0/24/3, 9/12/1, 30/6/4, 2/15/24

0	1	2	3	4	5	6	1	2
3	4	5	6	2	3	4	5	6

DECORATE A SNOWMAN

Players: 2
Object: The first player to finish a snowman is the winner.
Other Materials: Color crayons, scissors
Preparation: Cut out the number cards shown below.
To Play:
1. Mix up the cards and place them *face down* in a pile.
2. Each player takes 2 cards, multiplies, and finds the answer on the chart. The player draws on his or her snowman whatever goes with the answer.
3. If that part is already drawn, the player loses that turn.
4. Continue taking turns until someone has decorated a snowman with all 7 things.

Name _____

Name _____

hat	0, 8, 20
one arm	1, 10, 24
other arm	2, 12, 25
one eye	3, 9, 30
other eye	4, 15, 36
carrot nose	5, 18, 6
button	16, 12

0	1	2	3	4	5	6	1	2
3	4	5	6	2	3	4	5	6

© Instructional Fair • TS Denison

IF5204 *Math Practice Games Gr. 2*

✂ Addition Facts 0–10 ✂   Cards A

5 + 0	1 + 1	7 + 1	5 + 2	5 + 3	5 + 5
4 + 0	10 + 0	6 + 1	4 + 2	4 + 3	6 + 4
3 + 0	9 + 0	5 + 1	3 + 2	3 + 3	5 + 4
2 + 0	8 + 0	4 + 1	2 + 2	8 + 2	4 + 4
1 + 0	7 + 0	3 + 1	9 + 1	7 + 2	7 + 3
0 + 0	6 + 0	2 + 1	8 + 1	6 + 2	6 + 3

✂ Addition Facts 0–10 Reversed ✂   Cards B

0 + 5	1 + 1	1 + 7	2 + 5	3 + 5	5 + 5
0 + 4	0 + 10	1 + 6	2 + 4	3 + 4	4 + 6
0 + 3	0 + 9	1 + 5	2 + 3	3 + 3	4 + 5
0 + 2	0 + 8	1 + 4	2 + 2	2 + 8	4 + 4
0 + 1	0 + 7	1 + 3	1 + 9	2 + 7	3 + 7
0 + 0	0 + 6	1 + 2	1 + 8	2 + 6	3 + 6

✂ Numbers 0-10 ✂ Cards C

5	0	6	1	7	10
4	10	5	0	6	9
3	9	4	10	5	8
2	8	3	9	4	10
1	7	2	8	3	9
0	6	1	7	2	8

✂ Subtraction Facts 0–7 ✂ Cards D

2 – 2	4 – 1	5 – 2	6 – 2	7 – 1	7 – 7
2 – 1	4 – 0	5 – 1	6 – 1	7 – 0	7 – 6
2 – 0	3 – 3	5 – 0	6 – 0	6 – 6	7 – 5
1 – 1	3 – 2	4 – 4	5 – 5	6 – 5	7 – 4
1 – 0	3 – 1	4 – 3	5 – 4	6 – 4	7 – 3
0 – 0	3 – 0	4 – 2	5 – 3	6 – 3	7 – 2

✂ Subtraction Facts 8–10 ✂ Cards E

8 – 5	9 – 2	9 – 8	10 – 4	10 – 10	10 – 4
8 – 4	9 – 1	9 – 7	10 – 3	10 – 9	10 – 5
8 – 3	9 – 0	9 – 6	10 – 2	10 – 8	10 – 6
8 – 2	8 – 8	9 – 5	10 – 1	10 – 7	10 – 7
8 – 1	8 – 7	9 – 4	10 – 0	10 – 6	10 – 8
8 – 0	8 – 6	9 – 3	9 – 9	10 – 5	10 – 9

✂ Addition Facts 11–18 ✂ Cards F

4 + 7	6 + 6	7 + 6	7 + 7	6 + 9	9 + 9
5 + 6	7 + 5	8 + 5	8 + 6	7 + 8	8 + 9
6 + 5	8 + 4	9 + 4	9 + 5	8 + 7	9 + 8
7 + 4	9 + 3	3 + 9	4 + 9	9 + 6	7 + 9
8 + 3	2 + 9	4 + 8	5 + 8	5 + 9	8 + 8
9 + 2	3 + 8	5 + 7	6 + 7	6 + 8	9 + 7

✂ Addition 9+ Facts ✂   Cards G

9 + 6	9 + 3	9 + 9	15	12	18
9 + 5	9 + 2	9 + 8	14	11	17
9 + 4	9 + 1	9 + 7	13	10	16
9 + 3	9 + 9	9 + 6	12	18	15
9 + 2	9 + 8	9 + 5	11	17	14
9 + 1	9 + 7	9 + 4	10	16	13

Subtraction Facts 11–18

Cards H

11 – 4	12 – 6	13 – 7	14 – 7	15 – 6	18 – 9
11 – 5	12 – 7	13 – 8	14 – 8	15 – 7	17 – 8
11 – 6	12 – 8	13 – 9	14 – 9	15 – 8	17 – 9
11 – 7	12 – 9	12 – 3	13 – 4	15 – 9	16 – 7
11 – 8	11 – 2	12 – 4	13 – 5	14 – 5	16 – 8
11 – 9	11 – 3	12 – 5	13 – 6	14 – 6	16 – 9

✂ Numbers 0–33 ✂ Cards 1

0	1	2	3	4	5
6	7	8	9	10	11
12	13	14	15	16	17
18	19	20	21	22	23
24	25	26	27	28	29
30	31	32	33	Wild Card	Wild Card

✂ Numbers 34–67 ✂   Cards J

39	45	51	57	63	Wild Card
38	44	50	56	62	Wild Card
37	43	49	55	61	67
36	42	48	54	60	66
35	41	47	53	59	65
34	40	46	52	58	64

✂ Numbers 68–100 ✂ Cards K

68	69	70	71	72	73
74	75	76	77	78	79
80	81	82	83	84	85
86	87	88	89	90	91
92	93	94	95	96	97
98	99	100	Wild Card	Wild Card	Wild Card